BY AUTHORITY OF
THE LORD CHANCELLOR

AND THE SPEAKER O₁
THE HOUSE OF COMMONS

PARLIAMENT
AND THE
Glorious Revolution
1688 - 1988

On 13th February 1689, Prince William and Princess Mary of Orange met the 'Lords Spiritual and Temporal, and Commons' in the splendour of Inigo Jones' masterpiece, the Banqueting House in Whitehall. With solemn ceremonial, the clerk of the House of Lords read aloud the Declaration of Rights. Then, in the name of all the estates of the realm, the Marquess of Halifax requested that the Prince and Princess accept the crown. William's reply was direct: 'We thankfully accept what you have offered ... I shall do all that is in my power to advance the Welfare and Glory of the Nation'.

Thus was concluded the central event in the historical drama that was to become known as the Glorious Revolution of 1688–1689, when a king – James II, who claimed to rule by hereditary, even divine right – was deposed in favour of sovereigns, William III and Mary II, who occupied the throne by the will of the people as expressed through Parliament.

The influence of the Glorious Revolution is felt to this day. It has been a determining factor in the history of the United Kingdom for the last three hundred years. It has influenced the evolution of parliamentary government around the world. It laid the foundations of parliamentary democracy in Britain and still shapes the way in which Parliament conducts its business.

The Crown offered to William, 1689 *Silver medal cast by Anton Meybusch to commemorate the ceremony in the Banqueting House where William was offered the throne and guaranteed that he would preserve the liberties of the kingdom. The kneeling female figures represent England, Scotland and Ireland.*
(BRITISH MUSEUM)

The Roots of the Revolution

he roots of the Glorious Revolution lay in the conflicts of the reign of Charles I (1625–1649) which culminated in the Civil War, the execution of the king and the Interregnum, but which remained unresolved when the monarchy was restored in 1660. In constitutional terms, the central issue was – where did ultimate power lie, with the Crown or Parliament? Or, if sovereignty was shared between the two, what should be the balance of power?

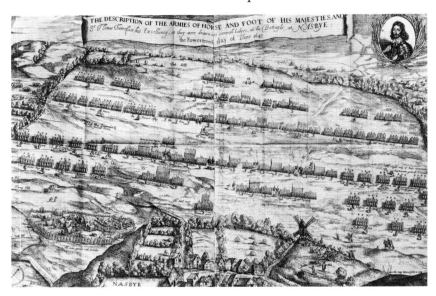

The Description of the Armies of Horse and Foot at the Battayle of Nasbye, 14th June 1645, from Anglia Rediviva by Joshua Sprigge *Naseby was the turning-point of the Civil War, a decisive defeat for the Royalist cause, after which recovery was beyond hope.* (MANSELL COLLECTION)

The execution of Charles I, 30th January 1649 *Charles I was tried for his life in January 1649 by a commission appointed by the House of Commons. He was beheaded on 30th January 1649 on a scaffold erected against the wall of the Banqueting House. By the dignity with which he met his death, Charles inflicted a massive propaganda defeat on his opponents and won for himself a martyr's crown.* (GUILDHALL LIBRARY)

The gloves worn by Charles I at his execution *The king gave the gloves to William Juxon, Bishop of London, on the scaffold.* (LAMBETH PALACE LIBRARY)

Under the Stuarts, the sovereign's hereditary right to succeed was understood as having been divinely ordained. It followed that kings owed their authority to God. Traditionally kings had prerogative powers which allowed them to intervene on occasions which were not otherwise provided for – such as pardoning criminals, or dissolving and summoning Parliament. But it was also understood that these powers should be exercised according to the 'laws and customs of the realm'.

The first Stuart king, James I (1603–1625), was convinced of his divine authority, and argued fiercely with his parliaments. However, he was too indolent to organise a powerful, centralised monarchy, and the Parliamentarians were too slow in pressing their claims against the Crown. His son, Charles I shared the same view of kingship but was more uncompromising in its application. Moreover, he was uncommunicative, stubborn and devious – characteristics which, whatever his true motives, created distrust of his aims and actions. The result was a series of increasingly severe confrontations between Crown and Parliament.

During the 1630s, Charles ruled without Parliament at all. In 1639, however, he blundered into a war with his Scottish subjects which by 1640 forced him to summon the legislature. In return for providing the king

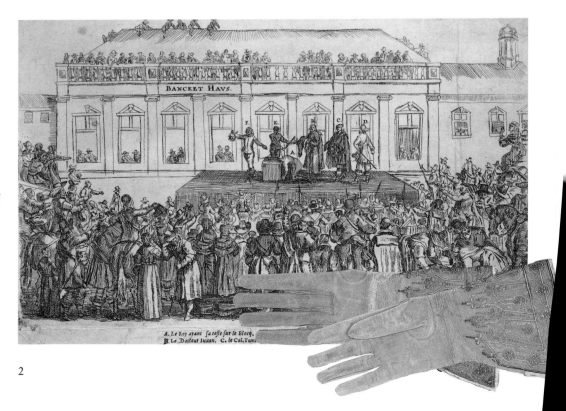

THE DEATH WARRANT OF CHARLES I

On 6th January 1649 the House of Commons passed an 'Act' appointing 135 commissioners to be a High Court of Justice to try King Charles I. In spite of many defections and of doubts about procedure, the court met formally for the first time on 20th January in Westminster Hall and by 26th, after hearing depositions from 33 witnesses, the commissioners had agreed amongst themselves to condemn the king to death. On Saturday 27th their sentence was pronounced in open court.

By then the death warrant had already been drawn up, with blanks for the time and place of the execution, which a committee was left to arrange. Some signatures – perhaps the first 28 – may well have been collected at that stage. Nothing could be done on the Sunday but, once the details of the execution had been approved on Monday 29th, the blanks were filled in and the warrant was taken into the Painted Chamber where the remaining signatures were added. Ultimately, 59 of the 67 commissioners who had pronounced judgment signed the warrant.

The story that Cromwell had to browbeat some of the commissioners into signing is unproven but certainly there had been a delay in settling arrangements which the warrant had not allowed for. It therefore became necessary to erase the dates and replace them with 'xxixth' January and 'uppon Saturday last'. Presumably also two of the original army officers to whom the warrant was addressed had refused to serve and the names of Hacker and Phayre were substituted. Other alterations may represent corrections to scribal errors though it is not clear whether Gregory Clement wrote his name over an erasure or whether his name was (incompletely) erased in 1652 because of his scandalous behaviour.

On 30th January Charles I went to execution on a scaffold erected outside the Banqueting Hall in Whitehall. The death warrant remained in Col. Hacker's possession until the restoration of Charles II in 1660 when Hacker, then a prisoner in the Tower of London, was ordered by the House of Lords to surrender the warrant to them. Since then the document has remained in their custody, at first in the Jewel Tower at Westminster, from 1851 on display in the House of Lords Library, and from 1979 in the Royal Gallery. Over the centuries it became worn and faded and even in 1800 it was 'not in a perfect state of preservation', but it is still fully legible under ultra-violet light. Unfortunately, even with the aid of a digital scanner, it is not possible to recover the words erased in 1649. On the back of the warrant is written in a seventeenth-century hand: 'The bloody Warr[an]t for murthering the King'.

The document is on a piece of parchment 43.8cm × 21cm. All the seals are of red wax, some of which are broken or obscured.

The reproduction is from a photograph by Geremy Butler

© *Crown copyright 1986*
First Published 1960
New edition 1986

Printed in England by Witley Press Ltd., Hunstanton for Her Majesty's Stationery Office
Dd 8814077   1/86

ISBN 0 11 700354 9

THE DEATH WARRANT
OF KING CHARLES I

HISTORIC PARLIAMENTARY DOCUMENTS

REPRODUCTION NO. 7

Published on behalf of the House of Lords Record Office
by Her Majesty's Stationery Office: 1986

25p net

with essential finance, the Long Parliament, as it became known, passed several acts designed to curtail the royal prerogative and to ensure that a Parliament should sit regularly and for reasonable periods. The king, however, made it clear that he regarded his concessions as only temporary and that he was willing to use force to defend his rights. Parliament responded by making progressively more radical demands, for example for control over the appointment of ministers. In a climate of growing mistrust, the two sides drew further and further apart, and gathered their own armies. Open warfare broke out in 1642.

By 1646, the forces of Parliament had triumphed and the king was their prisoner. Three years later, he was tried and executed. Kings had been deposed before and done to death. But never had an anointed monarch been publicly condemned for misrule and executed as a traitor in the name of the people. For the first time, the principle of the divine right of kings had been openly challenged.

With the death of Charles, the monarchy was abolished, along with the House of Lords and the Anglican Church, and, to all intents and purposes, the Commons had prevailed. But it was not an end. For four years, the country was governed by the Rump of the Long Parliament but it could not sustain its position. In 1653 the army seized control and, despite his honest attempts to persuade others to govern while he stood aside, for the next five years supreme power rested with the Lord Protector, Oliver Cromwell. Cromwell, however, was unable to establish a form of parliamentary government that would endure.

With his death, the republic collapsed, and the only acceptable alternative appeared to be a restoration of the old regime.

In 1660, after 20 years of instability and violence the country returned to the pre-war status quo, including a 'free Parliament'. Not only was the monarchy restored, in the person of Charles II (1660–1685), so were the House of Lords, including the Bishops, and the Church of England. But the tensions which had led to the Civil Wars had not been addressed. The Commons may have had a strengthened sense of its own power, imposing limits on the king by, for example, forcing him to dismiss unpopular ministers. But no new conditions were formally imposed on the king and the question of where power ultimately resided was still unanswered.

Cromwell dissolving the Rump of the Long Parliament, 1653 *The print records Cromwell as saying: 'Be gone you rogues, you have sat long enough'.* (BRITISH MUSEUM)

Bronze bust of Oliver Cromwell (1599–1658), after Edward Pierce, 18th century *A complex blend of country gentleman and professional soldier, social conservative and religious radical and political visionary, Cromwell towered head and shoulders over the politicians of the Interregnum. At one point he was offered the Crown – not to confirm but to limit his power.* (PALACE OF WESTMINSTER)

3

Restoration and Religion

Charles II shared the Stuart conviction that kingship was divinely ordained – no king touched so much for 'king's evil', the glandular disease that monarchs were reputed to be able to cure. Unlike his father, however, he was a shrewd and practical politician, who, while he would never compromise his principles, would sacrifice policies if it became necessary. It was a talent which enabled him to weather the severest political storms.

Charles II (1660–1685) by an unknown artist *Charles' reign was characterised by his determination to hold firm to his throne and his royal power. His mind was haunted by the bitterness of the Civil Wars, the execution of his father, and his own long years of penurious exile. He was determined 'never to go on my travels again'.* (NATIONAL PORTRAIT GALLERY)

When he came to the throne, Charles sought to build a regime on as wide a base as possible. Old royalists, moderate parliamentarians and Cromwellians all found places at different levels in government. The king also attempted a similarly broad-based restoration of the Church of England but with much less success.

At the beginning of the 17th century the Church of England stood unchallenged in authority. Even extreme Protestants worked within the Church and not against it. During the Civil Wars and the Interregnum, however, Anglicanism disintegrated. Its hierarchy had been abolished, its practices proscribed and its bishops had fled. A host of new Protestant sects had emerged – Presbyterians, Baptists, Quakers and other 'Dissenters'. Charles II sought to restore the Church of England with reforms that would make it acceptable to the majority of the more moderate Dissenters. He was unsuccessful. In Scotland the Covenanters resisted episcopacy while in England the Anglicans refused to accommodate Dissenters. Not only was the old Church restored in its entirety but in addition stringent tests of conformity were imposed that resulted, by the end of 1662, in a fifth of the clergy leaving the Church as 'nonconformists'. What is more, penal laws were introduced that placed severe restrictions on Dissenters.

In response, Charles several times sought to extend religious toleration to all non-Anglicans – Dissenters and Catholics alike. Again he failed. For many, the more extreme non-conformists were synonymous with the

A broadsheet appealing to Charles II to support the Anglican Church and eradicate Catholicism *The Pope is located in Babel, the source of confusion; the King in Bethel, the house of God. In the background are depicted the horrors of Catholicism.* (BRITISH MUSEUM)

BABEL and BETHEL: or, The POPE in his Colours.

WITH

The Church of ENGLAND's Supplication to his Majesty, our gracious Soveraign, the true Defender of the Faith; To protect her from all the Machinations of Rome, and its bloody Emissaries.

republicanism of the Interregnum and therefore to be suppressed. A greater fear however was of Catholicism. Since the Reformation, England had been a Protestant country. Only two per cent of the population, at most, were practising Catholics – 'recusants' who refused to attend services of the Church of England – and, while they were denied public office, by the time of the Restoration they were politically acquiescent. Nevertheless, one of the dominant themes of the period was anti-Catholicism which permeated every level of society and, however ill-founded, was a genuine fear. Decades of virulent Protestant propaganda had succeeded in convincing the great mass of the population that the Catholic Church was the most evil of heresies. And, moreover, that it was a religion which naturally led to, and sustained, arbitrary and despotic monarchies.

Given these fears, why then did Charles persist in seeking religious toleration? His motives are far from clear. Perhaps he was aiming to build a bloc of non-conformist support as a counterweight to Parliament. Perhaps, as Parliament suspected, he was attempting to revive his prerogative powers by suspending Acts of Parliament. Or it may simply have been that he was genuinely drawn towards Catholicism and wished to act in the interests of its adherents. Certainly, he inserted a secret clause undertaking to declare himself a Catholic 'at the appropriate time' into the Treaty of Dover which he concluded with Louis XIV of France in 1670. And it may well have been that, as some contemporaries feared, Charles did cherish despotic ambitions.

Whatever his motives, however, in 1672 Charles made one final attempt to achieve toleration by issuing a second Declaration of Indulgence which aimed to suspend the operation of the penal laws against Dissenters and Catholics. The result was to provoke Parliament into passing the Test Act. This provided that anyone holding a public office should openly receive the sacrament according to the Prayer Book and take the oath of supremacy and the declaration against transubstantiation. Practising Catholics were thereby forced out of office – and the most prominent casualty was James, Duke of York, the king's brother, who had been secretly converted to the Catholic religion in 1668. James resigned all his offices and then gave further offence to public opinion by marrying

again – his first wife having died in 1671. This time his bride was the devout francophile Catholic, Mary of Modena. The stage was being set for the most serious crisis of Charles' reign.

5 o o. thousand pound from Fra ce Yearly to Charls the 2 to keep the sitting of the Parlement of.

Playing Card: £500,000 p.a. from France to Charles II to keep the sitting of Parliament off *Under the Treaty of Dover, Louis XIV paid Charles substantial sums of money in return for his agreement to convert to Catholicism, to work towards the reconversion of England, and to join with France in a war against the Dutch. In the event, Charles only fulfilled the last condition but the French subsidies gave him significant freedom of action. These terms of the Treaty were secret but, as the playing card shows, news leaked out and engendered deep public suspicion.* (BRITISH MUSEUM)

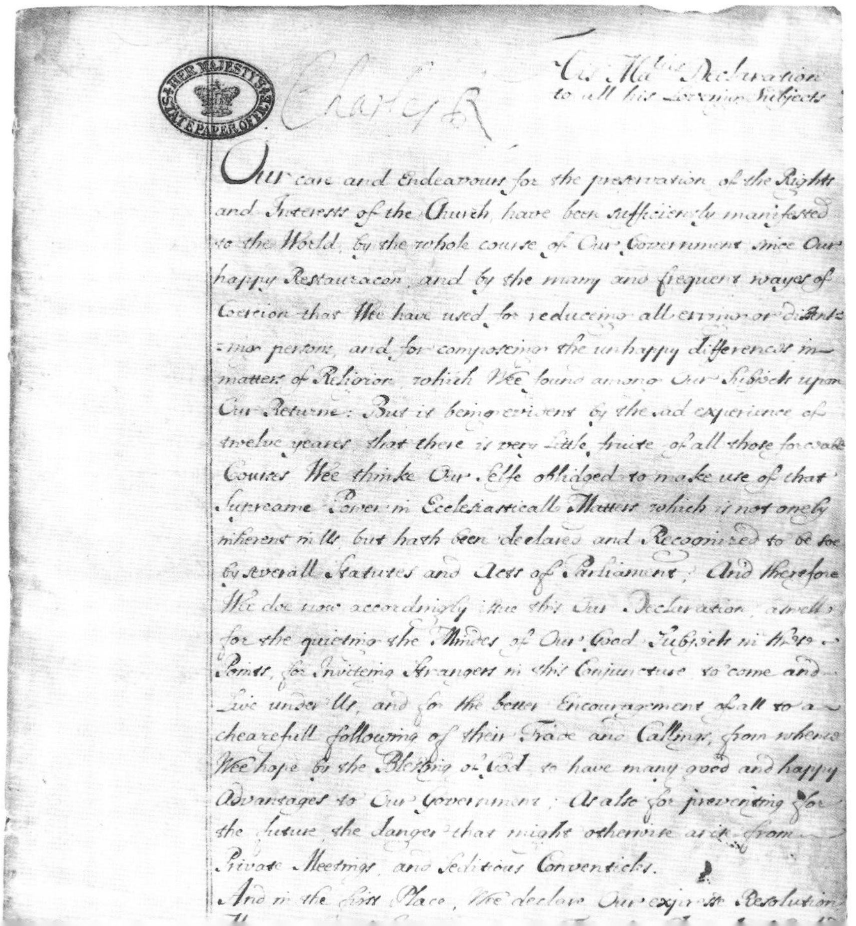

Declaration of Indulgence, 15th March 1672 *To many of his subjects, Charles' attempt to extend religious toleration to Catholics as well as Dissenters was part of a larger plan to create a Catholic despotism.* (PUBLIC RECORD OFFICE)

[Handwritten document, Declaration beginning "Charles R" and continuing:]

Our care and Endeavours for the preservation of the Rights and Interests of the Church have been sufficiently manifested to the World, by the whole course of Our Government since Our happy Restauration, and by the many and frequent wayes of Coercion that Wee have used for reducing all erroneous or dissenting persons, and for composing the unhappy differences in matters of Religion which Wee found among Our Subjects upon Our Return: But it being evident by the sad experience of twelve yeares that there is very little fruite of all those forceable Courses Wee thinke Our Selfe obliged to make use of that Supreame Power in Ecclesiasticall Matters which is not onely inherent in Us but hath been declared and Recognised to be so by severall Statutes and Acts of Parliament, And therefore Wee doe now accordingly issue this Our Declaration, as well for the quieting the Mindes of Our Good Subjects in these Points, for Inviteing Strangers in this Conjuncture to come and live under Us, and for the better Encouragement of all to a chearefull following of their Trade and Callings, from whence Wee hope by the Blessing of God to have many good and happy Advantages to Our Government; as also for preventing for the future, the danger that might otherwise arise from Private Meetings, and Seditious Conventicles. And in the first Place, Wee declare Our expresse Resolution

The Exclusion Crisis

During Charles II's reign, Parliament was much more in evidence than it had been before 1640. The Cavalier Parliament sat from 1661 to 1679, and there were three general elections between 1679 and 1681. And while Charles did not abandon attempts to pursue his own policies he was careful not to confront Parliament. In general, his approach was successful and although he suffered many political embarrassments and setbacks during his 25 year reign, there was only one major challenge to his authority – the Exclusion Crisis of 1678–1681, a full-scale attempt to subvert divine right and the hereditary succession by excluding James, Duke of York, from the throne.

Anthony Ashley Cooper, 1st Earl of Shaftesbury (1621–1683) *Like many of his class in the 17th century, Shaftesbury changed sides several times. At first a supporter of Charles I, he became in turn a prominent Cromwellian and then Charles II's Chancellor of the Exchequer and Lord Chancellor. But he maintained some consistent principles – support for free Parliaments, decentralisation and toleration for Protestant Dissenters; a hatred of standing armies and absolute monarchy.* (PALACE OF WESTMINSTER)

A True Narrative of the Horrid Hellish Popish-Plot, 1680, *a broadsheet which describes the main incidents of the Popish Plot in the style of strip cartoon. In the bottom left scene Oates is shown before the Council being questioned by the king.* (BRITISH MUSEUM)

The Crisis, which brought into focus all the latent anti-Catholicism in English society, was triggered by the Popish Plot, the revelations invented by Titus Oates that the Jesuits were planning to assassinate Charles and replace him with his Catholic brother. The story told by Oates was lucid and plausible, and made all the more convincing by the mysterious death of the investigating magistrate and the discovery of incriminating letters in the possession of James' private secretary. It provoked a wave of revulsion that was seized upon by the Earl of Shaftesbury to rally around him a party of opposition, willing to mobilise mass support and dedicated to excluding James from the throne. Charles was willing to make concessions to Parliament and had to sacrifice his chief minister, the Earl of Danby, who was impeached and sent to the Tower. But Charles would not compromise on his brother's hereditary right. Three times an Exclusion Bill was introduced into Parliament in 1679, 1680 and 1681, and three times Charles dissolved Parliament.

As part of his campaign, Shaftesbury organised a series of petitions in favour of Parliament in 1680. On the other side, loyalists expressed their abhorrence at such attempts to influence the King's prerogative to summon, prorogue or dissolve Parliament.

The 'Petitioners' and the 'Abhorrers' became in effect the first political parties. They soon attracted new titles – the derogatory terms 'Whigs' (Scots rebel Covenanters) and 'Tories' (Irish vagabonds).

The Whigs attracted town dwellers, Dissenters, and men without hope of royal favour; the Tories, the Church of England and the Court. Philosophically, the parties were distinguished by their differing attitudes to the nature of kingship. The Whigs subscribed to the view that royal authority derived from a contract that the king was understood to have made with his subjects, whereby he agreed to rule to their mutual advantage. The Tories endorsed the theory of divine right and the Anglican clergy went so far as to argue that, however arbitrary the monarch's behaviour, the subject had no right to resist.

A True Narrative of the Horrid Hellish Popish-Plot.

To the Tune of PACKINGTONS POUND. The Second Part

The Exclusion movement eventually failed because the odds were stacked in Charles' favour. The Whigs were fatally divided over who should replace James as heir – the Duke of Monmouth, Charles' illegitimate son, or Mary, James' Protestant daughter. And few Whigs were willing to contemplate violent action – memories of the Civil Wars were too strong. Charles, on the other hand, was able

Invariably flaws were found in the charters, they were declared forfeit and replaced by new charters which gave the king extensive powers over the choice of members of the corporation.

So, shortly after the monarchy had appeared to be tottering, Charles was able to enjoy his last few years on the throne in relative peace, and to hand over to his brother

to summon and dissolve Parliament as he chose, and use his majority in the House of Lords to defeat Exclusion time and again.

After three years, the Crisis subsided, as a substantial majority of the MPs who had been panicked by the Popish Plot took stock and decided that the dangers of a Catholic monarch were far outweighed by the potential threat to church and state posed by the Whigs. Throwing his full weight behind the Tories, Charles seized the chance to scatter his enemies. From 1681, Charles called no more parliaments. Whigs were dismissed from office in local government and replaced by Tories. Individual Whigs were prosecuted for treason and condemned by Tory judges and juries. Shaftesbury fled the country and died in Holland in 1683. In the same year, the Rye House Plot, a conspiracy by a few ex-Cromwellians to assassinate Charles and James, gave the government the opportunity to round up the remaining Whig leaders.

In order to gain royal control over the boroughs and the MPs they returned, a series of 'quo warranto' ('by what warrant?') proceedings were instituted against the charters which conferred the boroughs' privileges.

a secure Crown. Even James was surprised by the peacefulness of his accession. And when violence did erupt – in the form of risings in favour of Monmouth and Argyll – James' success in crushing them only served to strengthen his position.

The Execution of Monmouth and Argyll, 1685 *The silver medal, cast by R. Arondeaux, shows Justice standing over the fallen rebels.* (BRITISH MUSEUM)

17th century scythes said to have been used by peasants at the Battle of Sedgemoor, 6th July, 1685 *James, Duke of Monmouth, Charles II's illegitimate but Protestant son, had been deeply involved in the Exclusion campaign. In an attempt to seize the throne, he landed at Lyme Regis in June 1685 while his ally the Duke of Argyll landed in Scotland. Argyll failed to raise the Scots but Monmouth won a degree of popular support, mainly from peasants and miners. But his motley army was mown down at Sedgemoor. Both Monmouth and Argyll were captured and beheaded, and Monmouth's followers suffered under Judge Jeffreys' 'Bloody Assize'.* (ROYAL ARMOURIES)

King James II

ames II (1685–1688) was a man who saw the world in black and white. Like Charles II he espoused the divine nature of kingship but he possessed none of his brother's subtlety. Moreover, it was his overriding ambition to re-establish the Catholic Church in England. He honestly believed that once Catholics were relieved of their civil and religious disabilities, and were appointed to public office, there would be a mass return to the Faith.

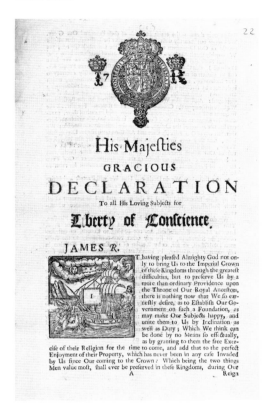

His Majesties gracious Declaration to all his loving subjects for Liberty of Conscience, 4th April 1687. (BRITISH LIBRARY)

James' accession was generally welcomed by the Tories who dominated the Parliament that gathered in 1685 since they saw in him the promise of firm government at home and peace abroad. They voted him revenues for life. They supported him against Monmouth. But when he proposed to repeal the Test and the other penal acts to enable Catholics to assume positions of responsibility, they refused to agree. What is more both Houses expressed concern about the way in which James was expanding his army and appointing Catholic officers whom he had dispensed from their legal disabilities. A standing army was the mark of an absolute ruler and at that very moment in France they had confirmation of all their worst fears of what an absolute Catholic monarch could do to his Protestant subjects. For at the same time as James was proposing toleration for Catholics in England, Louis XIV had revoked the Edict of Nantes which guaranteed political and religious rights to the Protestant Huguenots. And his army was forcibly converting the Huguenots to Catholicism.

Unable to secure its support, in November 1685 James prorogued what was probably the most pro-monarchist Parliament of the century and turned to non-parliamentary methods to secure his goals. On the one hand, he sought to appoint individual Catholics to public office. On the other, he aimed to forge a power base among Dissenters by freeing them from legal disability so that they could eventually form a dissenting Parliament able and willing to back him where the Tory-Anglicans would not.

In order to appoint Catholic office-holders, James used his prerogative to dispense them from the penalties of the Test Acts. But it was one thing to dispense individuals, it was quite another to issue dispensations for thousands of people. In April

James II by Sir Godfrey Kneller *Despite his failings and his ignominious end, James enjoyed a distinguished military and naval career before he succeeded to the throne. At the Restoration, he was made lord high admiral of England and twice commanded the English fleet in the wars against the Dutch. As a commander he proved himself a brave man and enjoyed a considerable measure of success. As an administrator he was capable, honest and industrious. But as a politician he was inept, unable to understand the motives or anticipate the actions of others. Those who opposed him he regarded as evil men deserving of punishment.* (NATIONAL PORTRAIT GALLERY)

8

1687, therefore, James issued his first Declaration of Indulgence, which suspended by royal decree all penal laws against Dissenters and Catholics, pending repeal by Parliament. James' immediate aims might have been limited to simply benefitting his co-religionists, but the implications of his actions were immense – for if the king could suspend some laws, he could threaten the entire legal system.

The same sense of menace accompanied James' next moves. In July 1687, he dissolved Parliament and began a campaign to pack a new House of Commons with Dissenters and Catholics, purging 'disloyal' members of municipal corporations, justice's benches and the lieutenancy, and – using the 'quo warranto' proceedings that Charles II had employed so successfully – substituting new borough charters for old so that councillors, who were often parliamentary electors, could be brought under royal control. In particular, he drew up a list of royally approved parliamentary candidates by ordering his agents to put the 'Three Questions' to Justices of the Peace: (i) would they agree to the repeal of the Test and penal acts if they were elected to Parliament; (ii) would they assist candidates so disposed; and (iii) would they accept the principle of religious toleration? For James, his actions were merely an extension of similar royal tactics in the past. For many of his subjects, they represented the thin end of the wedge. It seemed that royal power was being extended beyond traditional limits and that James was intent on turning Parliament into a mere rubber stamp for royal policies. Just as James had seemed to be threatening the law, he now seemed to be undermining the independence of Parliament.

The irony was that while James was alienating both Whig and Tory, he was failing to secure the support of the Dissenters, who, though they took advantage of the Declaration of Indulgence to worship openly, had great reservations about repealing the Test Acts since they feared that once in Parliament Catholics would set out to destroy Protestantism. In addition, Mary, James' Protestant daughter, and her husband William of Orange, let it be known that although they supported freedom of worship for all, they too were opposed to repeal of the Test Acts.

To James, however, his daughter's views were now largely irrelevant because, after 14 years of marriage, the queen was pregnant and

in June 1688 gave birth to a son. The thought of an heir to carry on a Catholic dynasty spurred James to greater efforts. But by the summer of 1688, it was clear that his policies were failing. In April 1688, he had issued his second Declaration of Indulgence which was ordered to be read in every church in the land. Seven bishops, including the Archbishop of Canterbury, presented a petition to James protesting against the order. In response, James had them brought to trial for seditious libel. Their 'rebellion' signalled the end of Anglican adherence to the doctrine of non-resistance to the Crown. Even moderate men were beginning to turn against the king. On 30th June 1688, the Bishops were acquitted to scenes of popular rejoicing. The same day seven Englishmen – both Whigs and Tories – sent an invitation to William of Orange to come and defend the liberties of England.

The Oxford Election of 1688 by Egbert van Heemskerk *As part of his campaign to pack Parliament, in March 1688 James II ordered the Corporation of Oxford to dismiss certain aldermen and to replace them with royal nominees. The Corporation voted to reject one of James' choices but was forced to succumb to the king in the end. The painting shows the scene in the Guildhall, with the Corporation jeering at the unpopular nominee. The bearer of the royal orders is at the back of the hall.* (OXFORD CITY COUNCIL)

The Seven Bishops *Silver medal cast to commemorate the action of the bishops against the Declaration of Indulgence. A large number of these medals were made, and worn round the neck, sometimes openly, sometimes concealed, by sympathetic clergy and lay people.* (BRITISH MUSEUM)

The Prince of Orange

illiam had already decided to invade England by the time he received the invitation. Indeed he had only been waiting to be 'invited by some men of the best interest' (Gilbert Burnet) before he took action. What had made up his mind was the imminent prospect of his wife's succession to the throne of England being frustrated by the birth of a son to James. What ultimately determined his move, however, was the international situation.

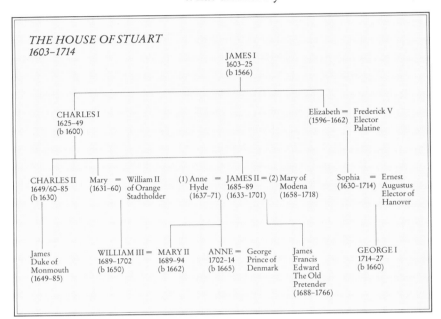

THE HOUSE OF STUART
1603–1714

JAMES I
1603–25
(b 1566)

CHARLES I
1625–49
(b 1600)

Elizabeth = Frederick V
(1596–1662) Elector
Palatine

CHARLES II
1649/60–85
(b 1630)

Mary = William II
(1631–60) of Orange
Stadtholder

(1) Anne
Hyde
(1637–71)

JAMES II = (2) Mary of
1685–89   Modena
(1633–1701) (1658–1718)

Sophia = Ernest
(1630–1714) Augustus
Elector of
Hanover

James
Duke of
Monmouth
(1649–85)

WILLIAM III =
1689–1702
(b 1650)

MARY II
1689–94
(b 1662)

ANNE =
1702–14
(b 1665)

George
Prince of
Denmark

James
Francis
Edward
The Old
Pretender
(1688–1766)

GEORGE I
1714–27
(b 1660)

The Revolution House, Whittington, near Chesterfield, from a banner produced to celebrate the centenary of the Revolution *The 'house' was the 'Cock and Pynot' (magpie) inn, where Danby and the Earl of Devonshire met in the autumn of 1688 to decide what action each should take in the event of an invasion by William. It was agreed that Devonshire would seize Nottingham for the Prince and Danby York.* (CHESTERFIELD BOROUGH COUNCIL)

Last page of the Letter of Invitation to William, 30th June 1688 *The invitation was sent by the Earls of Devonshire, Danby and Shrewsbury, Lord Lumley, the Bishop of London, Edward Russell and Henry Sidney. Their names are represented by the code numbers at the end of the letter.* (PUBLIC RECORD OFFICE)

William was Stadtholder of the Dutch United Provinces and his overriding concern was to preserve his country from attack by France, which he was convinced wished to conquer the whole of the Low Countries as a first stage in the domination of Western Europe. After 1685, more and more of his fellow countrymen came to share William's obsessive fear of France. Louis XIV's revocation of the Edict of Nantes, the maltreatment of Dutch merchants in France and the influx of Huguenot refugees all combined to create a sense of a Protestant country under threat from its powerful Catholic neighbour.

In William's eyes, the position of England was crucial to the future of his own country. If James secured a Catholic monarchy, there was every prospect that he would ally with Louis. On the other hand, if England could be brought into alliance with the Dutch, William could hope to fend off the French. For some years, therefore, William kept in close contact with the situation in Britain through a clandestine correspondence with a number of British politicians. And in 1687 and 1688, he sent his agents to discover what support he could expect. Then he suggested that he be sent an invitation 'to ... come and rescue the nation and the religion' (Burnet), and after it arrived, in the autumn of 1688 he issued a 'Declaration ... of the Reasons inducing him to appear in armes in the Kingdome of England ...' which set out the illegalities which James' evil counsellors had imposed, demanded an inquiry into the birth of James' son – whom it was said was not the queen's child – and acceded to the demand for a 'free Parliament'.

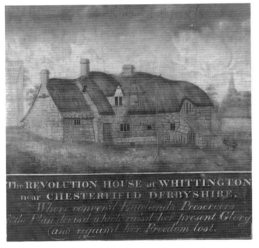

But in deciding to invade William was taking a huge risk. He could only set sail when he was sure that the French army was occupied elsewhere, and even then it was possible that Louis might strike before his return. The Dutch army numbered only 14,000 men compared with at least 20,000 under James' command. And it was bad strategy to begin a major naval expedition against the prevailing wind at the onset of winter. Such a risk was only justified by the expectation of rich rewards. Yet it is not clear whether, even at this stage, William was set on the Crown. He would probably have settled for less – a guarantee of his wife's claim to the succession and England's declaration of war against France.

Thomas Osborne, first Earl of Danby and Duke of Leeds (1631–1712) *Of the seven men who invited William 'to come and rescue the nation', one of the most influential was Danby, Charles II's chief minister from 1673 to 1678, when he was noted for his management of Parliament. Danby it was who had promoted the marriage of Princess Mary to William of Orange in 1677, and he had been one of the few Tories to openly oppose James II's policies. After William and Mary ascended the throne, he served as Lord President of the Council.* (NATIONAL PORTRAIT GALLERY)

Mary II (1689–1694) after William Wissing *The legitimacy of William's claim to the throne came through his marriage to James II's eldest daughter by his first marriage. A devout Protestant and a devoted wife, Mary contributed in no small way to the ultimate success of William's enterprise. By refusing to accept the Crown alone, she ensured that William would be made king. By sharing the throne with him, she brought many wavering Tories to accept the Revolutionary settlement.* (NATIONAL PORTRAIT GALLERY)

Once it became apparent to James that William meant to intervene in England's affairs, he suddenly reversed his policies. The campaign to pack Parliament was abandoned. Writs for a new Parliament were withdrawn and old borough charters restored. But by then it was too late. James' concessions made under duress won him no new support and he had surrendered the chance of summoning a new Parliament amenable to his wishes. Nevertheless, his regime was by no means on the point of collapse. Memories of the Civil Wars and more recently of the savage Bloody Assize which followed Monmouth's rebellion made it unlikely that there would be a rising. What is more, his army was large, professional and apparently loyal. Even if William did come, the odds were on James retaining his throne.

William first attempted to set sail on 19th October 1688 but was driven back by a storm. He put to sea again on 1st November. This time fortune favoured him. The 'Protestant wind' – as men came to call it – veered to the east, driving the Dutch fleet along the Channel and preventing James' considerable naval forces from leaving the Thames Estuary. On 5th November 1688, the anniversary of another deliverance from Popery – the unmasking of the Gunpowder Plot – William landed at Torbay. By February 1689, he had secured the throne.

The Timetable of Invasion 1st November – 22nd December 1688

THE ROUTE OF WILLIAM'S FLEET

NORTH SEA

ENGLAND

UNITED PROVINCES

Hellevoetsluis

Dover

Calais

TORBAY

SPANISH NETHERLANDS

ENGLISH CHANNEL

FRANCE

William's Departure from Holland by Lodolf Bakhuysen. (LORD IRONSIDE)

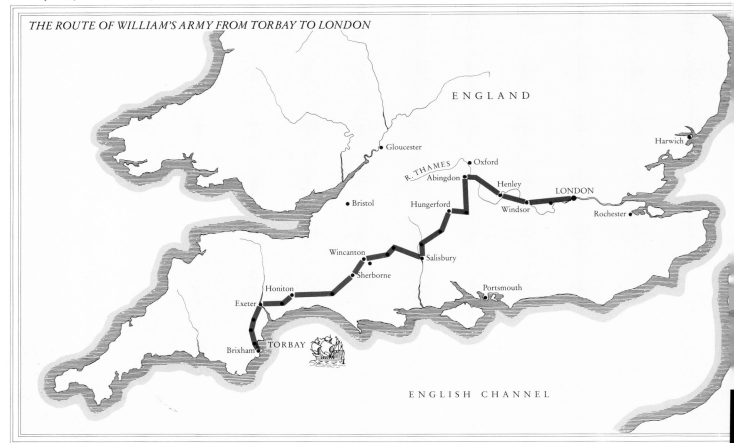

THE ROUTE OF WILLIAM'S ARMY FROM TORBAY TO LONDON

ENGLAND

Harwich

Gloucester

Oxford

R. THAMES

Abingdon

Henley

LONDON

Bristol

Hungerford

Windsor

Rochester

Wincanton

Salisbury

Sherborne

Portsmouth

Honiton

Exeter

Brixham TORBAY

ENGLISH CHANNEL

CHRONOLOGY OF EVENTS

November

1st   William's fleet sets sail.
2nd   William's fleet changes course for the
        south west.
5th   William's fleet lands at Brixham.
9th   William enters Exeter.
19th James joins his army at Salisbury.
22nd Skirmish between William's and James'
        troops at Wincanton.
        Nottingham, York and Newcastle
        secured for William.
        Churchill defects from James to William.
25th James' daughter, Anne, leaves London.
26th James returns to London. His army
        disintegrates.
        Bristol secured for William.

December

4th   William enters Salisbury.
7th   William reaches Hungerford.
8th   Commissioners from James meet
        William at Hungerford.
9th   The Queen and the Prince of Wales sail
        from Gravesend for France.
10/11th James flees from London and is
        captured at Faversham.
14th William reaches Windsor.
16th James returns to London.
18th James withdraws to Rochester.
        William enters London.
22nd James finally departs for France.

William of Orange landing at Torbay by an unknown artist. (REPRODUCED BY GRACIOUS PERMISSION OF HER MAJESTY THE QUEEN)

Harquebus armour belonging to James II *Made by Richard Hoden of London c1686, the armour bears the monogram 'I.R' for Iacobus Rex, King James.* (ROYAL ARMOURIES)

13

William Takes Control

nce William had landed on English soil, time was on his side. Disillusion with James was palpable. William made his way towards London slowly, waiting for the local gentry to join him and for James' forces to crumble. Apart from a few anti-Catholic riots in London and a few risings in the provinces, the country remained calm but tense. Politicians tried to preserve the forms of legality, partly to prevent the risk of disorder, partly, especially on the Tory side, to remove any pretext for deposing James, their anointed king.

The Restoration of the True Religion and Constitution in Great Britain, with the Departure of the Court and Family of King James II and his Queen from England, etc *A Dutch broadsheet that describes the main events in the fall of James from his calling of a free Parliament on 28th November 1688 to the moment of his arrival at his exiled court at St Germain on 1st January 1689.* (BRITISH MUSEUM)

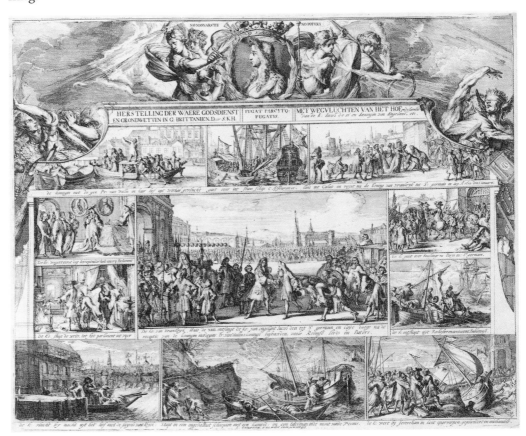

On 17th November, a group of peers and bishops petitioned James to summon a free Parliament so as to give William no further excuse to stay in England. James refused, preferring to trust to his army rather than put his fate in the hands of his subjects. Augmented by newly-raised regiments and others brought from Scotland and Ireland, James' army was a formidable force. But James' own indecisiveness prevented his engaging the enemy. He halted at Salisbury where incessant nosebleeds delayed him. By now his behaviour was becoming erratic and unbalanced and many of his professional commanders deserted his cause, including his protégé John Churchill, later Duke of Marlborough, and Prince George of Denmark, the husband of his second daughter Anne. Convinced that he could no longer rely on his troops, James ordered the retreat. And on returning to London he demonstrated that he had abandoned a military solution to the crisis in favour of a political one by issuing a proclamation summoning a Parliament for 15th January 1689.

He sent commissioners to negotiate with William at Hungerford. William's terms were not unduly harsh. He agreed to a Parliament

Address of the Lords assembled at the House of Lords to the Prince of Orange, 25th December 1688. (PUBLIC RECORD OFFICE)

THE

LORDS Spiritual and Temporal,

Affembled at the Houfe of LORDS, *WESTMINSTER, December* 25. 1688.

E the Lords Spiritual and Temporal Affembled in this Conjuncture, Do Defire Your Highnefs to take upon You the Adminiftration of publick Affairs, both Civil and Military, and the difpofal of the publick Revenue, for the prefervation of our Religion, Rights, Laws, Liberties and Properties, and of the Peace of the Nation; And that Your Highnefs will take into Your particular Care, the prefent Condition of *Ireland,* and endeavour, by the moft fpeedy and effectual means, to prevent the Dangers threatning that Kingdom: All which we make our Requefts to Your Highnefs to undertake, and exercife, till the Meeting of the intended Convention, the Two and twentieth of *January* next; in which we doubt not fuch proper methods will be taken, as will conduce to the Eftablifhment of thefe things upon fuch fure and legal Foundations, that they may not be in Danger of being again Subverted. *Dated at the Houfe of Lords,* Weftminfter, December *the Five and twentieth,* 1688.

summoned by James' writs but insisted that all Catholic officials should be dismissed and James' troops removed from London. But James was only buying time. He had no intention of calling a Parliament that might declare his son spurious. He sent his wife and son across to France, cancelled the parliamentary writs, and on the night of 10th December slipped away himself. For William no better outcome to the invasion could have been imagined. James had left of his own free will. No blame attached to William. But then James was captured by a group of fishermen and returned to the capital. Now clearly William had to ensure James' departure. Advised to leave London 'for his own safety', James took boat to Rochester and on 22nd December 1688 finally left for France.

Meanwhile, on 18th December, William had entered London and two days later summoned the peers to advise him on how best to call a free Parliament. About 60 members of the House of Lords assembled and on Christmas Day presented an Address inviting William to take on the administration of the country and to issue circular letters for parliamentary elections. Immediately after Christmas, some 300 men who had served as MPs in Charles II's parliaments met the Lord Mayor, aldermen and common councilmen of London and together concurred with the peers' advice. The next day letters were sent out to elect a Convention which was to decide how the country should be governed.

William III (1689–1702) attrib. Thomas Murray *William was shrewd, cautious, asthmatic and withdrawn – not the qualities to make him popular – but he was also tolerant, and not only in religious matters. In war and politics, he was obstinate in defence and courageous in attack, his life guided by a single fixed purpose – the defence of the Dutch nation. It was for this that he risked all in invading England.* (NATIONAL PORTRAIT GALLERY)

The Reception of H.R.H. the Prince of Orange at his entering London *The Prince is in the middle distance, his hat doffed.* (GUILDHALL LIBRARY)

The Convention Parliament

A part from the fact that no king summoned it nor read a Speech from the Throne, the Convention was in every respect like any other Parliament. Although it is sometimes difficult to define precise party allegiances, it seems that a majority of the House of Commons was Whig; the Lords predominantly Tory. Most Whigs had no difficulty in coming to terms with the idea of making William king given their fundamental belief that if a king broke his 'contract' with his people he could be deposed. The Tories on the other hand were unwilling to forsake the hereditary principle. The task of the Convention, therefore, was to reconcile these two opposing views.

Resolution by the House of Commons that James had abdicated, 28th January 1689 *The next day, the resolution was brought to the House of Lords, where on 30th January 1689 the word 'abdicated' was deleted and 'deserted' substituted in its place. 'Abdicated' was subsequently reinstated by the Commons and accepted by the Lords.* (HOUSE OF LORDS RECORD OFFICE)

The Convention first met on 22nd January but only began serious debate on the 28th when the House of Commons, articulating the Whig position, voted that James had violated the fundamental laws of the land and broken his original contract with the people, thereby abdicating the government and leaving the throne vacant. The House of Lords objected to the idea of the throne being 'vacant' since that implied that it was in the Convention's power to fill it, and substituted the more neutral 'deserted' for the word 'abdicated'. The reason behind the Lords' objections was that many of the peers – perhaps the majority – still hoped to keep James as king – either in name with William or Mary acting as regent, or in fact but with his freedom of action limited by conditions. They certainly did not feel able to elect a new monarch and indeed on 31st January voted against a proposal to declare William and Mary king and queen.

The Commons' original motion shuttled between the two houses for several days until William broke the deadlock. Mary having waived her claims to be sole ruler in favour of a joint sovereignty with her husband, William insisted on being given sole administrative authority. If not, he would leave England to solve its problems without him. Faced with this firm stand, the Lords eventually voted by a majority of almost 20 to accept the Commons' motion, salving their consciences by the possible ambiguity of the term 'abdicated'.

Meanwhile, the Commons had begun to discuss the issues which had precipitated the crisis. On 2nd February a committee headed by Sir George Treby presented a total of 28 'Heads of Grievances', a document which, after much discussion and redrafting, eventually formed the basis of the Declaration of Rights. Agreed by both Houses on 12th February, the Declaration was the formal statement of the Glorious Revolution. Largely the work of Whig committees, it nevertheless commanded general support since it was designed to appeal to Anglicans and Tories as well as to those radicals who wished to subordinate the royal prerogative to the Common Law and to enhance the status of Parliament.

The Declaration and the offer of the Crown were formally presented to William and Mary at a ceremony at the Banqueting House, under the magnificent Rubens' ceiling that asserted the divine right of kings. In April 1689, the joint monarchs were crowned.

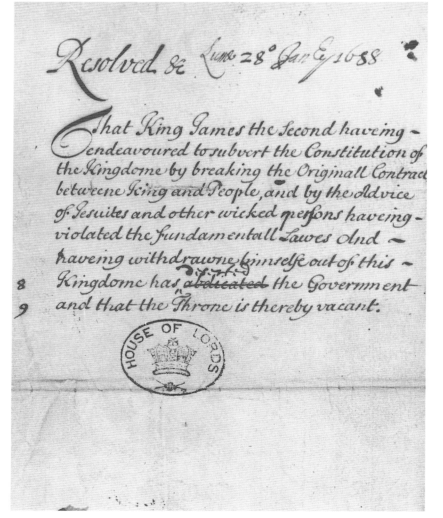

Resolved &c Lunæ 28° Janﬔ 1688

That King James the Second haveing endeavoured to subvert the Constitution of the Kingdome by breaking the Originall Contract betweene King and People, and by the Advice of Jesuites and other wicked persons haveing violated the fundamentall Lawes And haveing withdrawne himselfe out of this Kingdome has *deserted* abdicated the Government and that the Throne is thereby vacant.

The painting includes the major figures in the events of 1688–1689. To the right of Princess Mary are Thomas Wharton MP; Henry Powle MP, Speaker of the House of Commons, with his head averted; John Somers MP; Viscount Mordaunt and Sir Robert Howard MP. In front of Prince William kneels the Marquess of Halifax, Speaker of the House of Lords; and to the left of William are Bentinck, the Prince's closest adviser; Edward Russell MP; Danby; Lord Delamere; the Earl of Devonshire; the Deputy Clerk of the Parliaments; Churchill; the Bishops of London and Bristol; Gilbert Burnet; and Sir George Treby MP.

The Presentation of the Declaration of Rights by James Northcote *This was painted around 1789, at the time of the centenary of the Glorious Revolution.* (PALACE OF WESTMINSTER)

The text reads:
'This is certainly the greatest proof of the trust you have in us that can be given, which is the thing that maketh us value it the more and we thankfully accept what you have offered.

And as I had no other intention in coming hither than to preserve your Religion, Laws and Liberties so you may be sure that I shall endeavour to support them and shall be willing to concur in anything that shall be for the good of the kingdom and to do all that is in my power to advance the welfare and glory of the nation'.

The Prince of Orange's speech accepting the Declaration of Rights *The document is in Halifax's hand and dated two days after the ceremony in the Banqueting House. Although it contains the substance of William's speech, it represents the words – which Halifax wished to see – recorded in the journals of both Houses of Parliament.* (HOUSE OF LORDS RECORD OFFICE)

The Declaration of Rights

The Draft Declaration of Rights, 1689, the documentary centrepiece of the Glorious Revolution. The Declaration was in no sense an explicit contract between the ruler and the ruled. But, by its assertion of the rights of a free parliament and of the limits which should be placed on the operation of the judiciary, it marked the point when the balance of power finally tipped away from the monarchy towards Parliament.(HOUSE OF LORDS RECORD OFFICE)

he Declaration opened with a catalogue of those actions of James, such as dispensing with and suspending laws, which tended 'to subvert and extirpate the Protestant Religion and the Lawes and Liberties of this Kingdome', all of which were declared illegal. There then followed a statement that the throne was vacant – the implication being that this was a necessary consequence of James' illegal acts.

Next, the members of the Convention, aiming to define Parliament's future role, sought to create 'such an establishment as that their Religion Lawes and Libertyes might not againe be in danger of being subverted'. They then went on to assert thirteen essential rights. Seven were concerned with relations between Parliament and the king and either sought to prohibit the king from certain actions, such as levying revenue or maintaining a standing army in peacetime without parliamentary consent, or to assert the rights of Parliament regardless of the wishes of the Crown, for example, free elections, frequent parliaments and freedom of speech and debate. The six remaining rights consisted of the Anglican answer to James' attack on the Church, including condemnation of the prosecution of petitioners, namely the Seven Bishops, and of a number of reforms of legal abuses, notably 'that excessive Bayle ought not to be required nor excessive fynes imposed nor cruel and unusual punishments inflicted'.

Finally, the Declaration offered the throne to William and Mary – with the implication that the offer was conditional on their acceptance of the thirteen rights. It also set down the

The first page of the Declaration reads:

'The Declaration of the Lords Spiritual and Temporal, and Commons, assembled at Westminster.

Whereas the late King James the second, by the Assistance of divers Evil Counsellors, Judges and Ministers, imployed by him did endeavour to Subvert and extirpate the Protestant Religion, and the Laws and Liberties of this Kingdome.

By assuming and exercising a Power of dispensing with and Suspending of Lawes, and the Execution of Lawes without Consent of Parliament.

By committing and prosecuting diverse worthy Prelates for humbly petitioning to be excused from concurring to the said assumed Power.

By issuing and causing to be Executed a Commission, under the Great Seale, for erecting a Court called the Courte of Commissioners for Ecclesiasticall Causes.

By levying Money for and to the use of the Crown by the pretence of Prerogative for other Time and in other manner than the same was granted by Parliament.

By raiseing and keeping a standing army within this Kingdom in time of Peace without Consent of Parliament and quartering of Souldiers contrary to Law.

By causing several good Subjects being Protestants to be disarmed at the same time when Papists were both armed and Employed contrary to Law.

By violating the freedom of Election of Members to serve in Parliament.

By prosecutions in the Courte of King's Bench for matters and Causes Cognizable only in Parliament And by divers other Arbitrary and illegal Courses.'

line of succession – through the heirs of Mary, then the heirs of her sister Anne, and lastly the heirs of William.

The Declaration was not primarily concerned with individual rights nor was it a libertarian or democratic manifesto. It was a claim of the rights of Parliament against the Crown. In many ways it was a very conservative document which sought to prevent a repetition of the abuses of the past. It maintained the hereditary right to the throne and simply dealt with the awkward question of James' position by treating him and his son as if they were dead. But because William had to accept the Declaration when he accepted the throne and because, moreover, it defined the royal succession, it ensured that Parliament not the king would become the dominant partner in government.

The Declaration was passed into law as the Bill of Rights in December 1689.

The Engrossed Bill of Rights – the Declaration of Rights incorporated into the acts of Parliament, 16th December 1689 *In its final form the Bill of Rights is some seven feet long.* (HOUSE OF LORDS RECORD OFFICE)

The Coronation of William III and Mary II, April 1689 *This was the only true double coronation in English history.* (BRITISH MUSEUM)

Terracotta statuettes of William III, c1695, and Mary II, c1693. (VICTORIA & ALBERT MUSEUM)

The Constitutional Settlement

Three documents make up the constitutional settlement of the Glorious Revolution. The Bill of Rights with its assertion of the rights of Parliament in relation to the Crown. The Claim of Right (see pages 24–25) which fulfilled essentially the same function for Scotland. And the Act of Settlement of 1701. The Act was drafted in a time of peace in reaction to what was seen as William's high-handed conduct of government during the war against France between 1689 and 1697. Titled in full 'An Act for the further limitation of the crown and better securing the rights and liberties of the subject', the Act of Settlement failed to fulfil its grandiose promise since most of its articles were soon repealed or amended, such as the provision that holders of an office of profit under the Crown, or 'placemen', should not sit in Parliament. Three provisions, however, had enduring effect.

In the first place, the Act provided that a royal pardon should not be a bar to impeachment by Parliament, which further restricted the royal prerogative. Secondly, it asserted the independence of the judiciary by declaring that judges should hold their offices for life and could not be removed except by Parliament – a provision that still holds true. Above all, it settled the line of royal succession in accordance with the assertion of the Bill of Rights that 'it hath been found by experience that it is inconsistent with the safety and welfare of this Protestant kingdom to be governed by a popish prince'.

After the death of William and Anne, Queen Mary's sister, and any children they might have, the throne was to pass to the progeny of James I's daughter, Elizabeth, wife of the Elector Palatine, namely Sophia, Electress of Hanover, and her heirs, so long as they 'join in communion with the Church of England, as by law established'. A clear and exclusively Protestant line of succession had been created which has lasted to this day.

'Nova Progenies', A New Race from Heaven, Upper Hall, Royal Hospital Greenwich by Sir James Thornhill, completed 1725 *The Protestant successors of James II sought a fitting retort to the baroque splendours associated with their Stuart predecessors. In Thornhill's mural, George I (1714–1727), surrounded by his family, receives his sceptre from 'Peace'. A figure bearing the sword and scales of justice smiles down on him. 'Time' watches over a horn brimming with gold, and a figure symbolising the stability of the new order gestures towards Wren's great Protestant masterpiece, St Paul's Cathedral. Behind the king are his mother, the Electress Sophia of Hanover and the Princess of Wales. The armoured figure to the right is the king's son, the future George II, with 'Naval Victory' at his side. At the bottom of the painting, gesturing towards his work, is a self-portrait of Thornhill.* (WOODMANSTERNE)

nder the overall umbrella of Protestantism, late 17th century England was, in religious terms, a pluralist society. The Church of England's monopoly had never recovered from the ravages of the Civil War years despite the provisions of the Restoration of 1660, and dissenting sects flourished. The 'Heads of Grievances' drawn up by the Convention had spoken of 'uniting Protestants in the matter of public worship, as far as may be', but the move towards adapting the Anglican Church to suit the beliefs of non-conformists was stillborn. Instead, the Revolutionary Parliament, which was over-whelmingly Anglican, opted to confirm the established church while recognising religious pluralism as a fact of life by means of a Toleration Act.

The Religious Settlement

The Toleration Act of 1689 made no great claims for the virtue of religious toleration. It simply stated that 'some ease to scrupulous consciences may be an effectual means to unite their majesties' Protestant subjects in interest and affection'. In other words, it was a largely pragmatic move designed to secure wider support for the new regime and to reward the Dissenters who had supported the Revolution. It also reflected William's tolerant Dutch attitudes to Protestant dissent.

(303)

Anno Primo

GULIELMI & MARIÆ.

An ACT for Exempting Their Majesties Protestant Subjects, Dissenting from the Church of *England*, from the Penalties of certain Laws.

Ɒɼaſmuch as ſome Eaſe to Scrupulous Conſciences in the Exerciſe of Religion may be an effectual means to Unite Their Majeſties Proteſtant Subjects in Intereſt and Affecti- on, Be it Enacted by the King & Queens moſt Excellent Majeſties, by and with the Advice and Conſent of the Lords Spiritual and Temporal and the Com- mons in this preſent Parliament Aſ- Bbbb 2 ſembled,

The Act repealed none of the laws against religious nonconformity but exempted from the penalty of the law everyone who was willing to take the oath of supremacy and to declare themselves against Catholic beliefs such as the doctrine of transubstantiation. Dissenters were allowed to absent themselves from services of the Anglican Church and to worship freely so long as their meetings were notified to the authorities and the doors were not locked. Dissenting ministers were

allowed to preach freely provided they also subscribed to 36 of the 39 Articles that governed the Church of England – the articles excluded related to homilies, the consecra-tion of clergy and the right of the national church to prescribe ceremonies. The Act even took account of the Quakers' refusal to swear oaths and allowed them to *declare* their denial of papal authority and their belief in God the Father and Jesus Christ. The only people excluded from the benefits of the Act were Catholics, Jews and those who denied the divinity of Christ. And, Catholics apart, they were very few indeed.

In the wake of the Act, the number of dissenting meeting houses multiplied and freedom of worship for Protestants became a practical reality. Dissenters, however, remained second-class citizens since they continued to be excluded from public office and they still had to pay tithes in support of the Church of England, and this was to remain a source of discontent for many years. Like Catholics and Jews, they had to wait until the 19th century before they were able to enjoy full civic rights. On the other hand, the Act made England the most tolerant country in Europe next to Holland and practical toler-ation spread during the next hundred years as politics slowly lost its religious connotations.

Toleration Act, 1689. (HOUSE OF LORDS LIBRARY)

The Quakers' Synod, 1699 *A broadsheet hostile to the Quakers showing a meeting of Friends in progress.* (BRITISH MUSEUM)

The Financial
Revolution

The full impact of the Glorious Revolution derived not only from its specifically constitutional provisions but also from the changed relationship between executive and legislature that resulted from the Revolutionary financial settlement. Whoever controls the purse strings has held the balance of power between king and Parliament throughout the centuries. If the monarch was able to 'live of his own', he had no need to summon Parliament to vote extra supply or taxes. If he was dependent on Parliament for finance then Parliament had the opportunity to insist on the redress of grievances. Many members of the Convention were well aware that the royal finances were the key to securing the permanent seniority of Parliament in its relationship with the king. In the words of William Harbord: 'Can he whom you place on the throne support the government without the Revenue?' In the euphoria of the Restoration, Charles II had been granted the income from the customs and excise for life. In the wave of loyalty generated by the defeat of Monmouth, James II was granted the same. These 'ordinary revenues' gave the monarch the ability to govern without Parliament. In 1689 the Convention, which had turned itself into a Parliament by an act to which William gave his assent on 23rd February, determined to avoid the same mistake.

Although an enquiry in March 1689 demonstrated that the 'late' king's revenue and expenses had amounted to almost £2 million a year, the Commons resolved that William and Mary should have a guaranteed annual income of only £1.2 million – the traditional income of the monarch since the Restoration. A year later, Parliament granted the Crown the excise for life but the more valuable customs duties for only four years in the first instance. This was all part of a deliberate policy of restricting the king 'by keeping him poor, so that his poverty may necessitate him to call frequent Parliaments' (*Some Remarks upon Government*, Anon, 1689). And it was a policy that worked. The Crown could not now function on its ordinary revenues without the help of Parliament even in peacetime,

and Britain was at war from 1689 to 1697 and 1702 to 1713. The result was that during William's reign more taxation was raised than under any previous monarch and Parliament met every year.

The nature of taxation changed too. It became more regular and routine, notably through the Land Tax, and for this reason and because it was passed by Parliament, it became more acceptable to the populace at large. It was also becoming more controlled. For the first time Parliament began to consider the army, navy and ordnance estimates and appropriate specific revenues for their payment. And from 1691 to 1697 the House of Commons – which tried to exclude the Lords from matters affecting taxation – appointed a series of Accounts Commissioners to audit the resulting income and expenditure accounts and thus established the beginnings of a system of parliamentary financial control.

Despite the increases, however, taxation revenues proved inadequate to meet the demands of the wars against France, and the government had to resort to borrowing on an unprecedented scale. Kings had long been forced to borrow to meet short-term needs in a haphazard and unsystematic way, and lenders were rarely sure whether they would be repaid in full or at all. Under William, Parliament began considering various schemes for long-term borrowing. The most significant of these proved to be the Tonnage Act of 1694, under which subscribers to a loan of £1.2 million were guaranteed interest at 8 per cent from the receipts of the customs and excise, and were incorporated as the Bank of

Pages from 'A Briefe State of the Incomes and Issues of Their Majesties Public Revenue', 5th November 1688 – 29th September 1691. (HOUSE OF LORDS RECORD OFFICE)

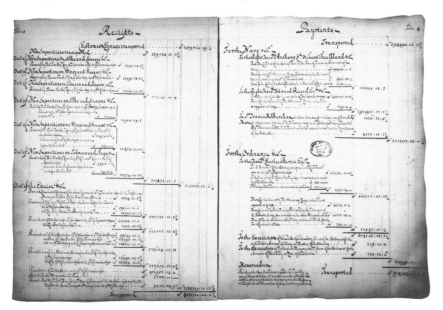

England and empowered to deal in Bills of Exchange. The knowledge that the interest on loans would be met from specific regular taxes guaranteed by regular parliaments gave small investors as well as the City the confidence to make long-term loans to the government and gave them an interest in the survival of the regime. By 1698 a national debt of over £5 million had been funded in this way and the monarch had lost his personal responsibility for the debts of the state.

The ability of Parliament to raise large tax revenues and to borrow on a large scale had two major consequences. It enabled Britain for the first time to wage war successfully against countries like France which were more richly endowed with natural resources. In the second place, it effectively destroyed the Crown's financial independence. The old distinction between ordinary and extra-ordinary revenues gave way to a new distinction between civil and military expenditure, and for the latter Parliament allocated the resources. This 'public revenue' was appropriated by Parliament for policies which it was persuaded were in the national, not just the dynastic, interest as was still the case on the Continent. The king still initiated foreign

policy but only Parliament could make it effective. Similarly, though the king and his ministers long retained control over the civil list, which covered the expenses of civil government including the Royal Household, the amount and source of the funds were fixed by Parliament. The king had become a paid servant of the state. Parliament had finally laid its hands on the purse strings and, although its grip weakened in the 18th century, it never quite let go.

A Room in the Bank of England, by M.Laurens, c1695 *A pen and ink drawing on vellum, showing a clerk at a desk and two merchants depositing money.* (BANK OF ENGLAND)

The 'Million Bank' Chest, late 17th century *The chest was used to hold the tickets of the 'Million Lottery', a financial scheme set up in 1694 as a means of raising funds for the war against France.* (PUBLIC RECORD OFFICE)

The Revolution
in Scotland

The Glorious Revolution was made in England and exported to Scotland. But, in many ways, the outcome in Scotland was much more radical, for not only did it entail the replacement of James by William and Mary, it also involved the complete overthrow of the political and religious settlement which had accompanied the Restoration of 1660. The Restoration had resulted in a greater degree of royal authority in Scotland than in England. It had also reimposed an episcopal established church on a nation with a strong Presbyterian tradition which had reached the height of its political influence during the Civil Wars. After the Revolution, the Crown's powers in Scotland were greatly curtailed, and episcopacy was abolished in favour of Presbyterian government of the Kirk.

Facies Arcis EDENBURGEENÆ The Southside of the Castle of EDINBURGH.

View of Edinburgh Castle from the south, by John Slezer, 1693 *In 1689, the castle was held by the Catholic Duke of Gordon and posed a serious threat to William's Convention of Estates.* (BRITISH LIBRARY)

The Claim of Right, 1689 *Among its articles, the Claim provided that no Catholic could accede to the Scottish throne or hold office; that the royal prerogative could not override the law; that the consent of Parliament was necessary for raising taxes; that Parliament should meet frequently and debate freely; and that torture, which had been admissible in Scottish law, should not be applied without evidence or in ordinary crimes. It also declared episcopacy to be a grievance.* (SCOTTISH RECORD OFFICE)

When, in September 1688, James II withdrew his troops to counter the threat from William, government in Scotland rapidly collapsed despite the efforts of the Scottish Privy Council. So, as soon as his position in England was secure, William invited the Scottish Lords in London to advise him on how to handle the situation north of the border. With only one exception, they counselled William to summon a Convention of Estates to meet in Edinburgh to settle the future government of the country.

The Convention was as representative as conditions allowed. William's supporters did not succeed in determining the composition of the Estates nor the outcome of their deliberations, and when the Convention met on 14th March 1689 no party had the upper hand. James' supporters, however, were weakened by their own divisions, and on 16th March, their cause was lost forever when the Convention received a letter from James threatening reprisals against those who defied his authority. His most active supporter, John Graham of Claverhouse, Viscount Dundee, tried to organise a rival convention at Stirling but found no backing and withdrew from Edinburgh leaving the field clear for those who favoured William.

William had hoped that developments in Scotland might follow the relatively conservative path adopted in England. But constitutional change proved unavoidable. On 4th April, the Convention resolved that James had 'forfaulted' the throne and thereby implied that there existed a clear contract between ruler and people. This was elaborated in the Claim of Right which the Convention accepted on 11th April and which placed significant legal and parliamentary limits on the Crown. On the same day William and Mary were proclaimed King and Queen of Scotland and shortly afterwards Commissioners were nominated to offer them the Crown on condition that they accepted the Claim of Right and the associated List of Grievances, although whether these instructions were carried out to the letter is unclear.

After the Convention was over, two matters remained outstanding – the exact nature of Parliament's relationship with the Crown and the question of the Church. Opposition to the government continued after the transfer of the Crown to William and Mary. And, following an unsatisfactory meeting of the Scottish Parliament in 1689, William was eventually obliged to agree to the abolition of the Committee of the Articles, the mechanism through which the Crown had exercised almost total control over parliamentary business. Thus in Scotland as well as England, the balance of power tilted from king to Parliament.

As far as the church was concerned, an Act of July 1689 had abolished 'prelacy' yet put nothing in its place. William would probably have preferred to retain the episcopate but in the event none of the Scottish bishops would transfer their allegiance from James. Thus William was forced to enter into an accommodation with the Presbyterians. In 1690 the Scottish Parliament abolished royal supremacy over the church and placed it in the control of the presbyterian ministers, some of whom had been dispossessed in 1661.

The Revolution in Scotland was not only distinguished by its radical nature but also by the fact that it provoked armed resistance. In April 1689, Viscount Dundee raised King James' standard. While he found little support in the Lowlands, he was able to muster a small force of Highlanders, who joined his cause perhaps less out of loyalty to the exiled king than from a traditional hostility to government. The rebels inflicted defeat on William's forces at the Battle of Killiecrankie in July. But, in the course of the battle, Dundee was killed and the next month his army was defeated at the Battle of Dunkeld. By the end of 1691, all the leading Highland Chiefs had submitted to the new government. Nevertheless, William's Scottish advisors felt the need to make an example of one clan. On 13th February 1692, Campbell regiments from Fort William, the military post established after Killiecrankie to impose Lowland domination on the Highlands, massacred the leader of the Macdonalds and nearly 40 men, women and children of his

clan in Glencoe. By then, the only force on Scottish soil actively supporting James was a small Jacobite garrison which had seized the island fortress on the Bass Rock in the Firth of Forth and which continued to hold out until 1694.

Violent and radical though it was, the Revolution nevertheless brought Scotland more in line with its southern neighbour than it had ever been before, despite the obvious differences between the two countries' ecclesiastical arrangements. By so doing, the Glorious Revolution largely made possible the Act of Union between England and Scotland which was eventually passed in 1707.

The Scottish Parliament from Atlas Historique by Henri Chatelain, 1718 *The Scottish Parliament was a single chamber assembly whose organisation and procedure differed from the Parliament at Westminster. In the ten years after the Glorious Revolution, its unstable politics encouraged many to see merit in a more easily managed single British Parliament.* (BRITISH LIBRARY)

The Articles of Union between England and Scotland, 1706 *The signatures of the English commissioners appointed to negotiate the union are in the left hand column, those of the Scottish commissioners in the right. The Articles, which passed into law in 1707, created a parliamentary and economic union but not the legal and ecclesiastical union that James I had wanted a century before.* (HOUSE OF LORDS RECORD OFFICE)

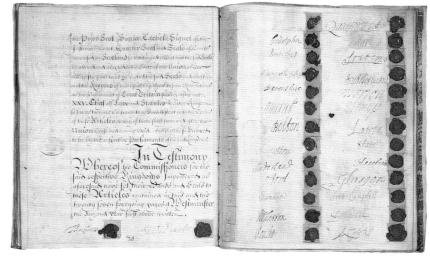

The International Dimension

he Glorious Revolution not only affected the destinies of the nations of the British Isles, it had a profound and permanent effect on Britain's relations with the wider world. Given that William's underlying motive for invading England was to secure the country's resources in his war with France, it is scarcely surprising that this should have been the case. But it is doubtful whether any of the men of 1688 foresaw how far-reaching would be the consequences of their actions. Certainly they could not have imagined that the repercussions would be felt not only on the Continent of Europe but eventually in North America and around the world.

Before 1688, the foreign policy of Cromwell, Charles II and James II had been primarily pro-French and anti-Dutch – the Dutch were, after all, England's main commercial rivals. The Dutch Wars, however, were of relatively short duration, and although the fighting did extend beyond the European theatre the campaigns were small-scale affairs. After 1688, on the other hand, France became an almost permanent enemy. Indeed, some historians have gone so far as to talk of a 'second Hundred Years War', stretching intermittently from 1689 to the Battle of Waterloo in 1815. While the description is misleading, since each of the Anglo-French wars had its own particular causes, there was one consistent thread running through the conflicts until at least 1745 – France's support for the Jacobite cause. In the Treaty of Ryswick of 1697, which ended the Nine Years War, Louis XIV agreed not to assist, directly or indirectly 'any of the Enemies of the said King of Great Britain'. However, on the death of James II in 1701, he formally recognised his son as James III and, until the defeat of Bonnie Prince Charlie's army at Culloden, French sponsorship of the Jacobites seemed to pose a serious threat both to English

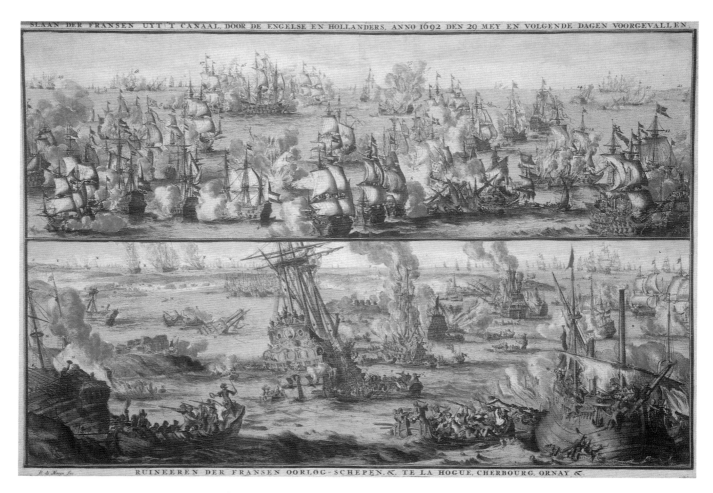

SLAAN DER FRANSEN UYT 'T CANAAL, DOOR DE ENGELSE EN HOLLANDERS, ANNO 1692 DEN 20 MEY EN VOLGENDE DAGEN VOORGEVALLEN.

RUINEEREN DER FRANSEN OORLOG-SCHEPEN, &c. TE LA HOGUE, CHERBOURG, ORNAY &c.

independence and the Protestant religion. It was this more than anything which made the English willing to sustain the huge military and financial burdens that the wars involved. The theme underlying the domestic struggles of the 17th century – fear of Catholic absolutism – now played a determining role in Britain's external affairs.

The wars against France were on a hitherto unprecedented scale. They were long and vastly complex in military and strategic terms. The Nine Years War (1688–1697) and the War of the Spanish Succession (1702–1713) were primarily European conflicts but the wars of 1744–1748 and the Seven Years War (1756–1763) represented a struggle for dominance in North America and India.

The F: King and ỹ K: of Spain with other Princes ingaging to root out ỹ Northen herisey.

That Britain was able to sustain its rivalry with France at this level was in large measure due to the Revolutionary financial settlement which put at the government's disposal the funds required. That the country was able to prevail in arms was largely the result of William's rebuilding of the army and the navy. William played a decisive part in the creation of the 18th century Royal Navy, its equipment, organisation and strategy, and left his successors an instrument of policy that could range the globe. The army he inherited in 1689 was inexperienced and demoralised by the

events of 1688. William reorganised it and stiffened it in battle, forging a weapon that would carry Marlborough to victory at Blenheim and Ramilles. But not only was the quality of the armed forces improved under William, their nature changed as well. The king was still responsible for their operation but ultimate control rested with Parliament which exercised its authority by passing the Mutiny Act on an annual basis and by providing finance a year at a time. Hence, Britain's army and navy ceased to be a predominantly royal preserve and became an expression of the national will.

By 1713, when the Treaty of Utrecht brought the War of the Spanish Succession to an end, Britain was able to negotiate with France as an equal. The nation that only a generation before had been little more than a pensioner of France had ended French dominance of Europe, emerged as a major force in European politics and established itself as a first-rate power on the international stage.

John Churchill, 1st Duke of Marlborough (1650–1722) by Sir Godfrey Kneller *Commander of the British armies under Queen Anne and the victor of Blenheim (1704), the turning point in the war against France, Marlborough had defected from James II to William in November 1688.* (NATIONAL PORTRAIT GALLERY)

Playing Card: The French King and the Spanish King engaging to root out northern heresy, 1689 *Issued as propaganda when England entered the Nine Years War (1688–1697) as a member of the Grand Alliance against France, the card sought to justify the war as a religious conflict.* (BRITISH MUSEUM)

The Influence of the Revolution

The Glorious Revolution not only had an impact on Britain and on Britain's relations with the other powers in the 18th century, it also played a significant role in the development of parliamentary government around the world. The political thought it generated influenced the American Revolution of 1776 and, to a lesser extent, the French Revolution of 1789. And the parliamentary arrangements to which it gave rise have helped shape the institutions of the many countries which have adopted systems of government on the Westminster model.

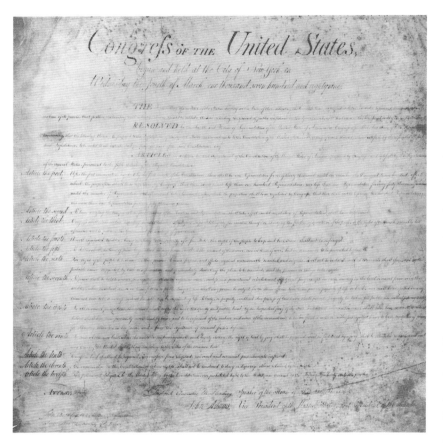

The United States Bill of Rights, 1789 *The American Bill of Rights has similarities with its English predecessor. In particular, article eight repeats article ten of the 1689 Bill of Rights almost verbatim – 'Excessive bail shall not be required, nor excessive fines imposed, nor cruel and unusual punishments required'.* (COMMISSION OF THE BICENTENNIAL OF THE U.S. CONSTITUTION)

In the American colonies, the Revolution in England created immediate repercussions, the most obvious being risings against the existing regimes in Massachusetts, New York and Maryland. Although the rebellions owed much to local grievances, there were general causes for repudiating Stuart rule in America – notably James II's attempts to bring the colonies together under a single imperial authority. The outcome of the risings also shared a feature in common – namely the assertion of the principle of representative government. Throughout the 18th century, the main tenor of politics in the colonies was for colonial assemblies to assert their power as against the executive and to demand the 'rights and privileges of Englishmen' in the manner of the English Parliament.

When Britain tried to impose more of the financial responsibility for maintaining the empire on the colonists in the period after 1763, the Americans viewed the moves as an attempt to overthrow their liberty much in the way that James II's policies had seemed an attack on English liberties 80 years before. And when the American Revolution finally erupted, the issues involved would have been very familiar to the participants in the Glorious Revolution: the proper distribution of governmental power, and the rights of subjects and citizens. Moreover, in making their new constitution the Americans drew on the English constitutional documents of 1689, notably the Bill of Rights, even to the extent of using some of the same phraseology.

The American Revolution was an inspiration to the French revolutionaries of 1789, and when they drafted their *Declaration des Droits de l'homme* they consciously followed the American Declaration of Independence. In the process, they were also harking back to the Declaration of Rights of 1689, a fact which some Frenchmen at the time recognised and which the Revolution Society in England was keen to point out.

Not that the influence of the Glorious Revolution on France was all filtered through the experience of the Americans. Many of the political thinkers of 18th century France, who had prepared the intellectual way for the Revolution, had looked directly to England for ideas and practical examples. Prominent among them was Montesquieu, who in his *Spirit of the Laws* made a celebrated analysis of the English constitution as it evolved immediately after the Glorious Revolution. For Montesquieu, English freedom rested on three main supports: the substantial 'separation' of executive, legislative and judicial powers; the 'mixed constitution' of monarchy, aristocracy and 'democracy' in Crown, Lords and Commons; and the system of 'checks and balances' which operated between these elements. Montesquieu's work had a formative effect on the constitution-makers of both revolutionary France and revolutionary America. Indeed, the concept of the 'separation of powers' is enshrined in the American constitution. But Montesquieu derived his ideas not only from observation and analysis, he also drew on the theories of John Locke, who provided the Glorious Revolution with its philosophical underpinning.

In his *Two Treatises on Civil Government*, published in 1690, Locke developed the contract theory of government which formed the basis of the Whig position in 1688–1689. Writing during the Exclusion Crisis, Locke sought to rebut the concept of a divinely ordained social order inherent in the theory of the divine right of kings by arguing that men in a pre-social state possess certain natural rights. In entering into a social state, that is in forming a government, they voluntarily sacrifice some of those rights in order to gain protection for the remaining ones. If rulers violate the natural laws, men, having freely made their contract with government, have a right to resist and if necessary dissolve the agreement.

Through the theories of Locke and the events of the French and American Revolutions, the ideas and issues raised by the Glorious Revolution became part of the mainstream of international political thinking. And their influence continues to resonate to the present day. Perhaps this is nowhere better illustrated than in the case of the 'Declaration of Rights'. The participants in the Glorious Revolution sought to justify

John Locke (1632–1704) by Michael Dahl *Locke was a member of the Earl of Shaftesbury's household in the 1670s and in 1687 joined the English followers of William of Orange in Holland.* (NATIONAL PORTRAIT GALLERY)

their actions by a written statement of the rights to which they believed themselves entitled. In the contemporary world, declarations of rights preface the constitutions of very many nations – even in some cases where those rights are not upheld in practice. In addition, international organisations have drawn up charters such as the United Nations' Universal Declaration of Human Rights and the Council of Europe's European Convention on Human Rights. Nowadays such statements are more concerned with the rights of the individual than with those of Parliament. But the impulse behind them, and often the very language they use, echoes the motives of the men of 1689.

The Execution of Louis XVI of France, 21st January 1793 *The French revolutionary Constitution of 1791 created a constitutional monarchy similar in some respects to that created in England by the Glorious Revolution. However, the untrustworthy behaviour of Louis XVI, notably his attempt to flee the country, and the political and social pressures occasioned by the outbreak of war against Austria and Prussia led rapidly to the abolition of the monarchy and then to the trial and execution of the king.* (MANSELL COLLECTION)

The Glorious Revolution and Parliament Today

he places where the influence of the Glorious Revolution is perhaps at its most tangible in the contemporary world are the modern British Parliament and those other parliaments, particularly in Commonwealth countries, which have derived their procedures from the Palace of Westminster. Naturally, Parliament in the late 17th and early 18th centuries was very different in many ways from Parliament today – not least because the Commons was not a democratically elected assembly. Nevertheless many of the developments in parliamentary practice that occurred in the decades immediately after 1689 are echoed in the way that Parliament conducts its business in the late 20th century.

Regular Parliaments and Frequent Elections

After the long periods during the reigns of Charles I, Charles II and James II when Parliament did not sit, the Bill of Rights insisted that 'Parliaments ought to be held frequently'. Since 1689, Parliament has sat every year and elections have been held on a regular basis. The Triennial Act of 1694 and the Septennial Act of 1716 provided for parliaments to last, first, for a maximum of three and, later, for a maximum of seven years, while present day parliaments have a maximum lifetime of five years. Annual sittings established Parliament as the centre of political power in Britain. Frequent elections made MPs more accountable to their electorates.

Freedom of Debate

Much of the monarch's power under the Stuarts derived from the way in which the king could harass and pressurise MPs and prevent them speaking out against abuses. The Bill of Rights specifically called for 'freedom of speech and debates or proceedings in Parliament'. After 1689, Members of Parliament were able to speak increasingly freely and to criticise what they saw as errors of policy or maladministration. Then, after the expiry of the Licensing Act removed censorship in 1694 – and even though the reporting of speeches was not officially allowed until 1771 – speeches in Parliament began to be reported in private prints and, later, in the press.

Today, freedom of speech is one of the most jealously guarded aspects of Parliamentary Privilege – those 'ancient and undoubted privileges' which the Speaker of the House of Commons claims at the beginning of each Parliament. It applies both to the Commons and Lords collectively and to individual members, and allows them to speak openly without fear of civil action.

Party Politics

Party politics is one of the most important features of modern British government. Political parties appeared in embryonic form during the Exclusion Crisis. They re-emerged under William and Mary and Queen Anne (1702–1714). But while the Exclusionists had been willing to turn to extra-parliamentary action, the 'Whigs' and the 'Tories' were now prepared to confine their rivalry within Parliament, with the Crown attempting to work with each of them in turn. The divisions between the Whigs and the Tories, however, were by no means as clear cut as

The House of Commons, 1708, by Peter Tillemans. (PALACE OF WESTMINSTER)

those between modern political parties. The 'Whig-Tory' divide was frequently undermined by divisions between 'Court' and 'Country' – the Court element consisting of those who sided with the king's ministers on any particular issue; the Country being made up of men who did not want power themselves but who insisted on their right to criticise those who exercised it.

Accountable Ministers

With the development of parties, in however nebulous a form, there followed the advent of ministerial accountability. Modern governments depend, in the final analysis, on securing the support of a majority of the House of Commons – in other words, of the 'back-benchers'. As the 18th century progressed and parties became more organised, so recognised leaders of the main groupings began to emerge, able to form administrations in effectively the modern manner and answerable to Parliament for their actions. By the 1720s Britain had acquired its first true Prime Minister: Sir Robert Walpole.

The Crown in Parliament

The constitution that the Glorious Revolution put in place subordinated the Crown to Parliament but retained a function for the monarch, who still chose ministers, and summoned and dissolved the legislature. In theory that arrangement still applies. Britain is governed by neither executive nor legislature alone but by the 'Crown in Parliament'. The history of the role of the monarchy in

politics since 1689, however, is the story of steadily diminishing effective powers. Queen Anne was the last monarch to reject a bill passed by both Houses of Parliament and after 1714 the sovereign rarely attended the House of Lords except on ceremonial occasions. The last three hundred years has seen the completion of the process which the Glorious Revolution effectively began – the transfer of political power to the representatives of the people.

An Election III: The Polling by William Hogarth, 1754. (SIR JOHN SOANE MUSEUM)

The House of Commons during the Administration of Robert Walpole, copy of a painting by Hogarth and Thornhill, 1730 *Walpole is shown standing at the left of the picture.* (PALACE OF WESTMINSTER)

Detail of Queen Anne in the House of Lords by Peter Tillemans, c1708. (REPRODUCED BY GRACIOUS PERMISSION OF HER MAJESTY THE QUEEN)

The Legacy of the Glorious Revolution

Historians have long debated the significance of the Glorious Revolution. A generation ago, for example, it was hardly seen as a revolution at all, merely a confirmation of the results of the Civil Wars. For Macaulay, the great 19th century historian, on the other hand, the country owed a debt of gratitude to events of 1688–1689 'for the authority of the law, for the security of property, for the peace of our streets (and) for the happiness in our homes'. Clearly such claims are exaggerated but there is no doubt that the Glorious Revolution was an historic turning-point.

The House of Commons, 1986, by June Mendoza *The artist has included not only the major figures of the 1983–1987 Parliament but also, in the gallery on the left of the painting, the ghosts of great Parliamentarians of the past. These include, reading from left to right, Aneurin Bevan, Cromwell, Lloyd George, Gladstone, Churchill and Disraeli.* (HOUSE OF COMMONS)

In the first place, by asserting that Parliament was the ultimate source of political power, it finally resolved the constitutional struggles of the 17th century. It set Britain apart from most of the rest of Europe where absolute monarchies seemed to be becoming the norm. And it laid the foundations of the parliamentary democracy of today. Secondly, by bringing Britain into alliance with Holland, it forced it into a conflict with France that was to erupt repeatedly throughout the 18th century, to spread across the globe and ultimately to transform Britain into a major power with a worldwide empire. The scale of the military and financial effort required by the war brought about profound changes in the conduct of administration, finance and politics. It also destroyed the last vestiges of the Crown's financial independence and confirmed the supremacy of Parliament.

In many ways, the Glorious Revolution was what would now be regarded as a typical British compromise. The changes the politicians of 1688–1689 made were restricted and pragmatic. They retained those elements of the past, notably Parliament, which preserved the tradition of government by consent. But by so doing they gave Britain a constitution with the flexibility to accommodate the great social, economic and political changes of the 18th and 19th centuries, and thus saved the country from the more bloody kind of revolution which other nations suffered.

Today, the influence of the Glorious Revolution continues to be felt – principally in the way in which parliamentary government is conducted not only in the United Kingdom but around the world. The hallmarks of parliamentary democracy – regular general elections, freedom of debate in Parliament and the press, the accountability of Ministers to Members of Parliament and of MPs to the electorate – all stem directly or indirectly from the momentous events of 1688–1689.